preparing for marriage

God's plan for your life together

Preparing for Marriage: Leader's Guide

© Pete Jackson/The Good Book Company 2007

Published by
The Good Book Company Ltd
Elm House, 37 Elm Road
New Malden, Surrey KT3 3HB, UK
Tel: 0845 225 0880; Fax: 0845 225 0990
email: admin@thegoodbook.co.uk
website: www.thegoodbook.co.uk

ISBN 13: 9781905564361

Printed in the UK

contents

introduction

The majority of people that many ministers prepare for marriage are not Christians. They may be attracted to you and your church because of the building, because of parental pressure, or because they have a vaguely-formed idea that being married in church is the 'proper' thing to do. For whatever reason they arrive at the door, there is both a responsibility for the minister to ensure that the couple are properly prepared for marriage, and an unmissable opportunity to explain the gospel to people who are lost without Christ.

Sadly, perhaps mainly because of the limited amount of time that pastors can give to marriage prep due to other time commitments, many churches are failing to fulfil *either* responsibility. We prepare people for the wedding day, but fail to have significant input into their marriage. And, because we sometimes feel awkward about preaching to a captive audience, the opportunity to explain the gospel slips out of our hands.

Preparing for Marriage is designed to help churches which are helping couples get ready for marriage to do both things within a limited time frame.

While not neglecting some of the practical aspects of marriage, *Preparing for Marriage* is unashamedly evangelistic. It is built on the premise that if people are not relating to God in a right way, they will not relate to each other in a right way—so talk of finances, chores, and even sex will, in the long run, be of little help. Some couples may think that they are already experts on these subjects—and could probably teach the minister a thing or two—this may well be true! But they will almost certainly know very little or nothing about the good news of Jesus Christ.

From Genesis 3 onwards, we see that without a right relationship with God, human relationships suffer. Sin breaks our relationship with God and also stops us from relating to our fellow men properly—including our spouse—regardless of how good at communication we are!

Undoubtedly, the best thing for all marriages is that both partners are committed to God through his Son, in whom we see what true love, self-sacrifice and forgiveness really are—the very qualities that build healthy, happy, stable marriages.

While not ignoring 'practical' aspects of marriage, *Preparing for Marriage* seeks to explain the gospel as the model for marriage. It also seeks to show that a relationship with God through faith in Christ is the very best thing for a couple as they embark on a lifelong commitment.

Why use Preparing for Marriage?

1. It's to the point. The best thing by far that a Christian minister can do for a non-Christian couple is to tell them the good news of Jesus. This is our primary task, and we ought to major on this. Many Christian ministers are not qualified (or not needed) to offer advice on the wide variety of topics that are often discussed on marriage prep courses.

While there is inevitably much which is not covered in a course of this length, the idea is to make the most of the opportunity that conducting weddings offers, and so make sure that couples are left with the gospel ringing in their ears, rather than just wedding bells.

2. It's short. When people come to a church to be married, the wedding legalities and a pretty building are usually all that they want from us. It is not unreasonable, and indeed part of our spiritual duty, to make marriage preparation obligatory. However, that being so, most couples would baulk at a course which was long, either in number or length of sessions. In addition, if your church building is in demand for weddings, too long a course will divert your energies from other ministries. *Preparing for Marriage* can be completed in four sessions of 30-45 minutes each.

You may like to have a meal together before the fourth session, which is a good time to discuss some of the practicalities of the marriage service. An optional fifth session can also be offered with a mature Christian couple who have been married for some time, in which to freely discuss any practical issue that is a concern for that particular couple.

3. It's relevant in a gospel-focused way. While majoring on the gospel, *Preparing for Marriage* has the integrity of being about marriage—it's not just an unwarranted 'preach' which ignores the real reason for the preparation. It makes the point that the gospel is good for marriage, and is actually the supreme model of how husband and wife are to relate to each other.

There are also very practical questions for couples to think through and discuss between sessions, which help to apply the Bible's teaching. So as we teach that marriage is the closest human relationship (a couple become 'one flesh'), the couple are encouraged to think through what affect this will have on other relationships with children, parents, or friends?

There are lots of good things we can do to help people prepare for marriage, but we must do the best thing. There is nothing better than explaining the good news of Jesus for making the most of the opportunity that weddings provide.

How to use Preparing for Marriage

Preparing for Marriage can be used with just one couple in a home over a cup of coffee; or with lots of couples together in a group setting, in a church hall, say.

In these notes I have included suggestions for how the course might work out with a single couple one-to-one (121) or in a group setting. However, the 'start up exercise' should only be used for groups if you are confident doing it, and if you are sure that the people doing the course (especially the blokes) will be comfortable with it. If people feel awkward or embarrassed or put on the spot they, understandably, won't want to return. For most people, it will be strange enough coming to a group like this—let's not make it more difficult than it need be! If you are in any doubt as to whether these exercises are suitable for your group, it is best, having welcomed people and discussed anything raised by the previous session, to crack on with the talk, in which they are free just to listen anonymously.

During the talk, there are times when you will read the Bible (from the Study Guide). It's probably best to do this yourself—certainly in the first session. If you can be sure that the people you are doing the course with can read comfortably, and would not be embarrassed by reading in a group context, then you may like to invite someone to read the Bible verses. You'll have to gauge for yourself whether this would be appropriate—but I would err on the side of caution, as usually, people don't like to be put in the spotlight in an unfamiliar context. In addition, the reading of God's Word is the most important part—so it's important that it is read well.

At the beginning of the first three sessions, there are a few questions for each couple to think through (after Session One you can encourage them to think about these in advance). You could still give a few minutes at the beginning of each session for further thinking (or initial thoughts if they didn't get round to it in the week), while you sort out the drinks! Make sure you have pens available. Encourage the couple to talk about their answers with each other, before discussing them with you.

At the first session, you may like to begin by outlining the structure of the sessions so that they will know what to expect and how things will work eg: 'We will usually start with a few questions to think about, I will give a short talk followed by an opportunity for you to ask any question you like.

When it comes to the time for the talk, point out in the study guide the summary of the material you are about to cover, along with the relevant Bible verses, before you begin the talk.

I have included a full transcript of the talks as I deliver them to give you a guide to how it could be done, but do, of course, feel free to make it your own—inserting your own illustrations and insights. It will always come across more personally, and with more conviction, if you spend the time doing this. If you want to listen to how I deliver them, you can listen online at www.thegoodbook.co.uk (search for Preparing for Marriage).

At the end of the talk, encourage them to take a couple of minutes to think through what has been said, and then encourage discussion by inviting them to make any comments or ask any questions that they may have.

May God bless you with insight, courage and sensitivity as you share this material with couples on the brink of marriage. And through it, may the Lord Jesus, who gave himself for his bride, be glorified.

Pete Jackson
March 2007

a marriage made in heaven?

1 Study Guide

Write down:

★ What was it that first attracted you to your future wife/husband, and what attracts you to them now?

_____

_____

_____

_____

★ What do you think is best about them?

_____

_____

_____

_____

★ Why do you want to get married?

_____

_____

_____

_____

how it all started

GOD THE CREATOR...

- of men and women
- of everything
- of marriage

MARRIAGE...

- ...for one man and one woman...
- ...for life

GOD...

- made everything and is therefore in charge
- can be known by us because he has spoken
- has even shown us what he is like in Jesus

Questions for discussion:

★ *What do you think of God's blueprint for marriage?*

_____

★ *Has anything you've heard today surprised you?*

_____

_____

★ *If God made everything (and everyone), how should people treat him?*

_____

_____

Genesis 1 v 26-28

[26] Then God said, 'Let us make man in our image, in our likeness, and let them rule over the fish of the sea and the birds of the air, over the livestock, over all the earth, and over all the creatures that move along the ground.' [27] So God created man in his own image, in the image of God he created him; male and female he created them. [28] God blessed them and said to them, 'Be fruitful and increase in number; fill the earth and subdue it. Rule over the fish of the sea and the birds of the air and over every living creature that moves on the ground.'

Mark 10 v 6-9

[6] At the beginning of creation God 'made them male and female.' [7] 'For this reason a man will leave his father and mother and be united to his wife, [8] and the two will become one flesh.' So they are no longer two, but one. [9] Therefore what God has joined together, let man not separate.

Colossians 1 v 15-16

[Jesus] is the image of the invisible God ... For by him all things were created: things in heaven and on earth, visible and invisible ... all things were created by him and for him.

Mark 4 v 35-41

[35] That day when evening came, he said to his disciples, 'Let us go over to the other side.' [36] Leaving the crowd behind, they took him along, just as he was, in the boat. There were also other boats with him. [37] A furious squall came up, and the waves broke over the boat, so that it was nearly swamped. [38] Jesus was in the stern, sleeping on a cushion. The disciples woke him and said to him, 'Teacher, don't you care if we drown?' [39] He got up, rebuked the wind and said to the waves, 'Quiet! Be still!' Then the wind died down and it was completely calm. [40] He said to his disciples, 'Why are you so afraid? Do you still have no faith?' [41] They were terrified and asked each other, 'Who is this? Even the wind and the waves obey him!'

to think about together...

1 Marriage is the closest relationship between two human beings—they become 'one flesh'. How will this affect or change your relationship with:

- any children you may have?

- your parents or parents-in-law?

- brothers, sisters, best mates?

2 What boundaries will you need to set for these other relationships?

3 How will you make sure that you grow closer together as a couple, rather than get stale or drift apart?

TOP TIPS

Here are some ideas that others have found helpful:

★ Spend half an hour every day talking together—each ask the other about their day, worries, hopes, plans, frustrations, etc.

★ Plan to spend two uninterrupted hours alone every week—just enjoying one another—having fun together!

★ Every few months or so, plan a day away by yourselves.

★ Find an activity that you can do together.

★ Plan to eat together

★ If you have children, try to have two or three days away together on your own once a year.

Discuss with your partner how you can put these ideas into practice.

For next time: Talk through the issues on this page, and fill in and discuss your answers to the questions opposite.

a marriage made in heaven?

Leader's Guide

Welcome

121

- Greet the couple and put them at their ease.

- Give them each a copy of the *Study Guide*, and explain that you will be working through it in the following weeks.

- If you have not already done so, establish the date and time of your subsequent meetings, and the date of the wedding.

group

- Try to make an effort with the set-up of the room—simple flowers on the tables, music playing as people arrive and appropriate refreshments. If you are working with several couples, seat them at separate tables, or in groups of four.

- As above, but get the participants to introduce themselves to each other. You might like to use this standard ice-breaker. Get one partner to introduce their future spouse to another couple. Then shout out information that they have to give without looking or asking. Colour of eyes; what they are wearing; birthday; favourite film, food, activity; football team they support etc. This should produce some laughs, may cause a riot, but also raises an important initial question. How well do they actually know the person they are about to commit their whole lives to?

Opening

Start by answering the following questions from page 5 of the booklet:

★ *What was it that first attracted you to your future wife/husband, and what attracts you to them now?*

★ *What do you think is best about them?*

★ *Why do you want to get married?*

These are important issues to establish at the start. Many couples arrive at wedding prep with inadequate answers to these questions. It is not unusual for some (usually men) *never* to have told the other that they love them!

Answers to these questions should be discussed openly and honestly, and where appropriate, you should encourage them to put things right straight away. I know one minister who orders the blokes to have the 'I love you' conversation there and then—and leaves the room for 10 minutes!

Session 3 defines what true love is for men in particular—self sacrificial commitment—so it is important not to give in to the way many women might define love—as a romantic feeling. If the questions create a stir, then ask: *'What do you most want for your partner?'* as a follow-up question. If the answer is *'the best; to be happy; etc.'* then you can encourage them that, even if they cannot, hand on heart, talk about deep feelings, then what they are expressing is actually true love.

Handling the responses and implications of these first questions in a group is much more difficult. These things certainly need to be explored, perhaps in a private interview when you meet to discuss the practicalities of the ceremony. From the front in a group setting, you should encourage couples to plan an evening when they can talk these things through in the week following.

Talk

The Big Idea: God is the creator of everything (including marriage), and everyone (including us). He is therefore in charge, and established the pattern for how married life should be.

Introduction

I think it's brilliant that you want to get married. You've decided to have a Christian wedding in church, and I think that's brilliant too!

This little course intentionally looks at both marriage and the Christian faith side by side because, as I hope you'll see, the Christian faith is all about a marriage—marriage between God and his people—and in particular between Jesus and his followers (Christians; the church). It is that relationship which is the model for the marriage between a man and a woman.

During our four sessions together we're going to consider both the wonderful things about marriage, and also the hard things—the things that can make marriage difficult. We're also going to think about the best way for you to live your married life together. I'm going to encourage you to talk together about a number of practical things in between these sessions. We'll also consider the promises that you're going to make on your wedding day, and there will be the opportunity for you to discuss any aspect of marriage that you want to.

But, as with most things, the best place to start is the beginning, so in this first session we will look at the origins of marriage, which we're told about in the Bible...

> ⬎ **READ: Genesis 1 v 26-28 and Mark 10 v 6-9**
> *(on p 7 of the Study Guide)*

God the Creator...

The first thing to say is that God is a God of relationships—you can see that in v 26, where he says: *'Let us make man in our image.'* It becomes clear later in the Bible that God the Father, God the Son, and God the Holy Spirit were working together in creation. And because God is a relating God, he made us for relationships too—a relationship with Himself and relationships with each other. So marriage was God's idea from the very start...

Verses 27-28 tell us that a special relationship between one man and one women was set in place at the beginning of creation. It involves them leaving their families, being united to one another, and becoming one flesh. This is an important phrase. It refers both to sexual union, and to the fact that this is a permanent relationship. Which is why Jesus warned that *'man should not separate them'*—a challenge that I will repeat to everyone in the church after you have made your vows. This very special, lifelong relationship is what we call 'marriage'. It means that there is no such thing as a trial marriage, because marriage is permanent, and by nature, a trial is not—so a trial marriage is impossible.

But hang on a moment, you might say! Looking at the origins of marriage is all very well, but surely this is just speculation? How can we really know anything about God—how can we know that he even exists?

Let me ask another question: How can we know anything about anyone? How do you know anything about each other? Answer: You have to speak. And if you hadn't spoken when you first clapped eyes on each other, then you wouldn't know each other, and you certainly wouldn't be here today on the brink of getting married.

It's the same with God. If God has not spoken then he can't be known, and what people say about him (and his view of marriage) is just a guess. But if he has spoken, then he *can be* known.

The very first chapter of the Bible says that God is a speaking God. As early as v 3 we're told: *'And God said: "Let there be light", and there was light'.* That first chapter of the Bible goes on to tell how, at God's word, all creation came into being: stars, oceans, plants—everything—even human beings. The message is very clear—you name it, God made it.

Now I want you to imagine making something yourself—perhaps a small wooden table or a clay vase. You've made it, so it's yours—you own it. Basically, you're in charge of it and you get to decide what happens to it—whether to keep it yourself, give it to your fiancée, or smash it up. You call the shots because it's yours.

Well, because God made the world (and us), we all belong to him and he's in charge. That means that he has the right to be in charge of both the world and our lives.

I wonder if you've ever thought of God like that. That's the Bible's view of him—not an old man with a long beard sitting on a cloud, but the Almighty Creator of everything (including you and me), who is actually in charge of us all, and who has spoken so that he can be known.

Obviously, it's one thing knowing something about someone, but a very different thing knowing them personally. Some people dream of marrying a super-model or a hunky film star. A few become obsessed and write them letters or hang around outside their millionaire mansions, hoping to catch a glimpse of their 'dream partner.' Of course, they can stand outside and write all the letters they want, but their only chance of having a personal relationship with a super-model or a film star is if that famous person decides to come out of their mansion and speak to them. It's the famous person who must take the initiative—it's up to them not you!

Well, in the person of Jesus, God has stepped out of his mansion, and come down to meet us. Listen to what another part of the Bible actually says about Jesus:

❯ READ: Colossians 1 v 15-16 *(on p 7 of the Study Guide)*

That's why Christians take Jesus so very seriously. He's the one who shows us what God is like. He's the image of the invisible God—he is, as someone put it: 'God with the skin on'. And you can see that in what he did... Colossians 1 tells us very clearly that he is the Creator of all things—he's the one responsible for all the creating that we're told about in Genesis 1. So if we want to know what God is like, we must look at Jesus.

And a quick look at Jesus' life backs up this incredible claim: he healed the sick, raised the dead, fed thousands of hungry people with a single packed lunch—and he showed amazing authority over creation.

> READ: Mark 4 v 35-41 *(on p 7 of the Study Guide)*

You can tell it was a bad storm because experienced fishermen believed that they were about to die. They woke Jesus up, and he did an extraordinary thing: He basically stood up and told the wind and the waves to calm down and shut up! He spoke to them... and instantly they obeyed him.

Speaking to the wind and waves would probably be enough for you or me to be locked away. But when Jesus does it, they obey—it's not a problem for the one who made them. And Jesus' friends, who were first terrified of the storm, are now afraid of Him—they realise they are in the presence of true greatness and awesome power. Look at what they say in v41b: 'Who is this? Even the wind and the waves obey him!'

Well, that's a brilliant question—who is it that has such great power? Genesis 1 tells us that God is the one who speaks and creation does exactly what he says. The same thing happened when Jesus spoke. Who could Jesus be, other than the God of heaven?

When God finished creating everything, we're told that he saw that it was good. The world was a great place and people related both to God and to other people in the right way (no arguments or fights)—it was brilliant! But you don't need me to tell you that the world is not like that now—currently 40% of marriages end in divorce, and of those that survive, many are only relationships of convenience. What on earth has gone wrong? We'll find out next time!

Questions for discussion:

★ *What do you think of God's blueprint for marriage?*
★ *Has anything you've heard today surprised you?*
★ *If God made everything (and everyone), how should people treat him?*

Refer the couple(s) to the questions in the booklet (p 6), and field the questions they raise. If you are running the course in a group setting, you could get them to discuss the questions in groups of four, and then feedback answers after a few minutes. Better to note the questions and promise to return to them in a subsequent session, than to over-run on the first session.

Homework

Encourage each couple to meet during the week specifically to talk through the questions and tips on page 8. Also encourage them to work through the initial questions on page 9 so that you can get off to a flying start next week!

Your notes

Your notes

Your notes

the problem with marriage

Write down:

★ *What do you think will be difficult in marriage?*

_____

_____

_____

★ *What is it about you that will make being married to **you** difficult?*

_____

_____

_____

★ *What is it about your partner that will make being married to them difficult?*

_____

_____

_____

★ *Why do you think these things might be a problem?*

_____

_____

_____

the heart of the problem

ALL PEOPLE...

- Think they know better than God, and so ignore Him while living in His world.

- Think they are in charge and so put themselves first.

- Think they are okay with God,
  but are actually guilty of rebelling against Him.

SO WHAT?

- Our world and lives are messed up.

- We are in a broken relationship with God.

- God will judge and make sure justice is done.

- God will punish all who are guilty.

- The punishment is being cut off from God forever ('hell').

Questions for discussion:

★ *What did you think God thought of you before today (or what did you think about yourself)?*

_____

★ *Has anything you've heard today surprised you?*

_____

_____

★ *Do you agree or disagree that you are a rebel in God's world?*

_____

_____

Genesis 2 v 16-17
[16] And the LORD God commanded the man, 'You are free to eat from any tree in the garden; [17] but you must not eat from the tree of the knowledge of good and evil, for when you eat of it you will surely die.'

Genesis 3 v 1-6
[1] Now the serpent was more crafty than any of the wild animals the LORD God had made. He said to the woman, 'Did God really say, "You must not eat from any tree in the garden"?' [2] The woman said to the serpent, 'We may eat fruit from the trees in the garden, [3] but God did say, "You must not eat fruit from the tree that is in the middle of the garden, and you must not touch it, or you will die."' [4] 'You will not surely die,' the serpent said to the woman. [5] 'For God knows that when you eat of it your eyes will be opened, and you will be like God, knowing good and evil.'

[6] When the woman saw that the fruit of the tree was good for food and pleasing to the eye, and also desirable for gaining wisdom, she took some and ate it. She also gave some to her husband, who was with her, and he ate it.

Romans 3 v 10-12
[10] As it is written: 'There is no-one righteous, not even one; [11] there is no one who understands, no one who seeks God. [12] All have turned away, they have together become worthless; there is no one who does good, not even one.'

Hebrews 9 v 27
Man is destined to die once, and after that to face judgement.

to think about together...

The main problem with marriage is that we are all sinful (self-centred, rebels against God)—and this directly affects all our relationships.

In marriage, our freedom to be self-centred is seriously restricted. We are no longer able to do just what *we* want, but must consider the needs and desires of our partner. Conflict is almost inevitable!

1. *What are the things most likely to cause conflict between you?*

2. *How, as a couple, do you resolve conflict at the moment?*

3. *How do you think you could improve conflict resolution?*

4. *When is the best time to resolve difficulties?*

5. *What are you like at backing down and saying sorry?*
   What are you like at accepting an apology and forgiving?

TOP TIPS

Discuss the merits of the following 4 ways of dealing with conflict:
- ★ **Going on the attack** (forcing my opinion on my partner)
- ★ **Passively submitting** (just agreeing to keep the peace)
- ★ **Cutting a deal** (each give and take a little)
- ★ **Negotiation** (what is best for you both as a couple).

The biggest areas of conflict in marriage are:
- ★ **Money**—how it is organised and spent
- ★ **Children**—how many, when, and sharing the care workload
- ★ **The wider family**—how much and how often will you see them?

If you haven't done so already, you need to talk through each of these areas and be sure that you understand any different attitudes you may have.

Discuss with your partner how you can put these ideas into practice.

the problem with marriage

2

Leader's Guide

Welcome

121

- Check that the couple have discussed the material on pages 8 and 9 of the Study Guide. It may have raised important issues that they want to discuss with you.

group

- As a start-up exercise, you could ask couples to discuss marriages that they know that have failed, and marriages that have 'succeeded' in their view. Why do they think these marriages failed? Irrespective of what actually happened, what personal qualities led to their downfall? By contrast, what personal qualities do they think lead to lasting marriage?

Talk

The Big Idea: Sin—our selfish desires, and rejection of God—wrecks relationships. It destroys our relationship with God. It can destroy your relationship with your partner.

Recap: Last time we saw that God made everything and everyone—which means He's in charge. We also saw that God is in the business of relationships. He made men and women for relationship, both with himself and each other.

Marriage involves one man and one woman leaving their homes, and being joined together for life—becoming 'one flesh'. The phrase 'one flesh' describes the closest possible relationship that two human beings can have, and it is expressed in sexual union.

And that is why divorce is so painful—because two people who have become 'one' are ripped apart. They are like two pieces of paper that have been glued together and then pulled apart a week later—both are damaged. Obviously, no one enters into marriage thinking that it is going to fail. But we have to be realistic about this.

Ian and Kelly were married in August. By March, one of them was 'seeing' someone else. By the following July, they were no longer living together and shortly after their first wedding anniversary, Ian discovered that Kelly was living with someone else.

Imagine for a moment how you would feel if you were in Ian's shoes and your future husband or wife suddenly turned their back on you and was unfaithful to you. It would be terrible. A friend of mine was physically sick for days when her husband of two and a half years confessed to having not one, but several, adulterous relationships. They were so in love only 24 months earlier, but now they were so far apart. Why is it that our hopes, dreams and our best intentions work out so badly?

When God finished making the world, we're told that he saw that it was good. Clearly, the world is far from good now, so what on earth has gone wrong?

> **READ: Genesis 2 v 16-17 and 3 v 1-6**
> *(p 11 of the Study Guide)*

Creation was completely good. But Genesis 3 tells us that it didn't stay that way for very long. And the essence of what went wrong was a relationship breakdown.

You see, the man and the woman did exactly what God said they should *not* do—they thought they knew better than God. They actually tried to be God by deciding for themselves what was right and wrong. Basically, *they* wanted to be in charge in God's world.

But, remember from last time, that God the Creator is really in charge, so it's not surprising that he won't put up with that kind of behaviour.

The end of Genesis 3 tells us that God kicked them out of the garden. They had turned their backs on him, and so now their relationship with him is broken. In addition, as a direct result of a broken relationship with

God, their own relationship has, for the first time, become strained—and causes the husband and wife to have the first ever 'domestic'!

Now what has that got to do with us? Well, the Bible tells us that turning our backs on God is what is wrong with us too—and, as with the first man and women, it leads to our own relationships being messed up—including our marriages.

> **READ: Romans 3 v 10-12** *(p 11 of the study guide)*

The word 'righteous' simply means 'right with God'. And Romans 3 tells us that *no one* is right with God: 'There is no one righteous, *not even one*'. It goes on to tell us that no-one seeks God and that all have turned away from him.

God made us. He loves us. He is in charge of us. But we have done the most damaging thing imaginable in a relationship: we have turned our backs on him and walked out. And then, we carry on living our lives as if he isn't there, and worse, flirting with other gods. That is, we make something or someone else the focus of our lives.

The Bible word for all this is 'sin'. It simply means turning our backs on the God who made us, and who is really in charge. It's as if we say to God: 'I know better than you... leave me alone... I'm not interested in you... I want to live *my* life *my* way'. It's a terrible way to treat God—living in His world, enjoying what he has made and given to us... and ignoring him.

I wonder if you can see how this affects us? For the first husband and wife back in Genesis, a good relationship with each other actually depended upon a good and right relationship with God—they didn't fight until they turned their backs on God.

In the same way, our own inclination to live 'my way' and ignore God will have a huge impact on marriage. We put ourselves first—which at some point, probably sooner rather than later, creates tension and division between us as we seek to get your own way—and the things you wrote down at the beginning may help you to see where that tension might come for you. The reason for all those things is that we are all 'sinful'.

People usually think that they're okay—quite good really compared to most others. But the Bible says that none of us is good—we've all ignored

God. Have a look at v 10: 'There is *no one* righteous, *not even one*'; v 11 'There is no-one who understands, no-one who seeks God'; and v 12 'All have turned away'.

It's a pretty grim picture of human beings. I wonder if you've ever considered yourself as someone who has turned your back on God. How we do that is seen in different ways and in varying degrees… greed, theft, hatred, murder, rape, immorality, lying, cheating, gossip, envy, dishonesty, and plenty more besides. Of course, some people look better than others, but the Bible insists that inside, we are all self-serving rebels against God.

So what? Well, for a start, our world is messed up because we ignore God. You only have to take a brief look at the TV news on any day of the week to see what our world and communities are like… selfishness, vandalism, fraud, people starving, war crimes and so on. But marriage is a major casualty of this spiritual disease we all have—people just give up when it gets tough. Britney Spears infamously gave up within 24 hours before it even had a chance to get tough! These are all marks of a world full of people who have turned their backs on the God who made them.

I wonder what you would do if you were God and the people you had made ignored you and lived as if they were in charge?

❯ READ: Hebrews 9 v 27 *(p 11 of the Study Guide)*

This verse tells us exactly what God is going to do. One day God will judge everyone. How do you think you'd fare if you met God today and he judged you? We may not like the idea that God will judge us, but judgment is part of our society, and we all want justice—which is why there is a public outcry when criminals seem to get off lightly.

Even young children want justice—they often cry: 'It's not fair'. Justice is ingrained in us all—we all want it, except when it is directed at us! And as far as God is concerned, we are all guilty rebels. So when you and I meet God, and he wants to bring justice to bear, we are in big trouble. We are guilty. We deserve to be punished.

The Bible explains that the punishment for ignoring God is being cut off from him forever (sometimes called 'hell'). In this, God is being perfectly fair and letting us have our way: we choose to live without him in life, so he will let us live in eternity without him. And that means without all the good things he made for us to enjoy... fun, food, family, friendship, football, fishing, whatever.

Although you might not think it now, the fact that God judges shows that he cares about us. If he didn't care, he wouldn't do anything, and people could do just as they please (bully, gossip, murder, steal etc.) without any fear of judgment. God's love for us means that justice must be done, but we've got to remember that we are all guilty too.

Thankfully, this is not the end. There is some really good news to come back for next week—I hope you will! Today has been bad news about our relationship with God and bad news for marriage. But it's always good to know the bad news because then something can be done about it. And it's important to enter marriage with our eyes open. Two selfish sinners living together, trying to grow together, is bound to create problems. Next time we'll find out what God has done and how that has a wonderful impact not only on our relationship with him but also on our marriage relationships.

Questions for discussion

★ *What did you think God thought of you before today (or what did you think about yourself)?*
★ *Has anything you've heard today surprised you?*
★ *Do you agree or disagree that you are a rebel in God's world?*

Discuss their responses to these questions.

Homework

• Encourage each couple to meet again during the week to talk through the questions and tips on page 12.

• Tell them also to write down separately their answers to the questions on page 13, and then discuss them together before you next meet.

Your notes

Your notes

Your notes

the sacrifice 3 *of marriage*

Write down:

★ *What personal qualities will you bring to this marriage?*

- _____

- _____

- _____

★ *What sort of husband / wife do you think you will be?*

_____

_____

_____

_____

★ *What are your expectations for your husband/wife? (What do you want from them?)*

_____

_____

_____

_____

_____

the model for marriage

LOVING SACRIFICE

- Jesus was selfless—even to death

- Jesus took the 'rap' for the way we have treated God (Jesus was punished for our sin in our place).

- Jesus was cut off from God so we don't have to be.

SO WHAT?

- God must love you very much to let his Son die for you.

- Jesus' death opens the way for us to come back to God and be forgiven by him—and not get what we deserve for ignoring him (for being 'sinful').

- We can't 'sit on the fence' regarding Jesus.

Questions for discussion:

★ *Did you realise how much God loves you?*
What is remarkable about the love he shows us at the cross?

_____

_____

★ *Why do you think Peter emphasises that Jesus was 'righteous' (never did anything wrong)?*

_____

_____

_____

Ephesians 5 v 25

[22] Wives, submit to your husbands as to the Lord. [23] For the husband is the head of the wife as Christ is the head of the church, his body, of which he is the Saviour. [24] Now as the church submits to Christ, so also wives should submit to their husbands in everything. [25] Husbands, love your wives, just as Christ loved the church and gave himself up for her.'

Mark 15 v 22-25, 33-34

[22]They brought Jesus to the place called Golgotha (which means The Place of the Skull). [23]Then they offered him wine mixed with myrrh, but he did not take it. [24]And they crucified him. Dividing up his clothes, they cast lots to see what each would get. [25]It was the third hour when they crucified him.

[33]At the sixth hour darkness came over the whole land until the ninth hour. [34] And at the ninth hour Jesus cried out in a loud voice, 'Eloi, Eloi, lama sabachthani?'—which means, 'My God, my God, why have you forsaken me?'

1Peter 3 v 18

Christ died for sins once for all, the righteous for the unrighteous, to bring you to God.

to think about together...

1. *What do you think makes your future spouse feel loved?*

2. *How will you sacrificially serve each other?*
What will your love for each other mean that you have to give up?

3. *What habits or behaviour in yourself should you seek to change for the sake of your spouse and marriage?*

4. *Sex is the ultimate expression of giving of self to your spouse. How might sex become selfish? How will you aim to avoid this?*

TOP TIPS

★ Tell each other what you respond to most... words (compliments, thanks, encouragement), actions, surprises, gifts, touch, time together or something else.

★ Don't make assumptions about the jobs that you do around the house—cleaning, cooking, laundry, DIY, gardening and accounts. Work out how these tasks will be done together, and *express your gratitude to each other* for doing them.

★ Recognise that change can be extremely hard! Some of our bad habits and attitudes are deeply ingrained, and your partner will need encouragement to keep working at it.

★ Don't keep affection just for the bedroom! Loving talk, touching, listening, holding hands and all that stuff should be a normal part of your married life together. It builds trust and closeness.

the sacrifice of marriage

Leader's Guide

Welcome

- Check that the couple have discussed the material on pages 12 and 13 of the Study Guide. It may have raised important issues about character and any weaknesses they might have. The study on sin could expose issues of trust between couples that will need very sensitive handling.

group

- As a start-up exercise, you could ask couples to talk about something that they had to give up, and how difficult they found it—smoking, drinking, computer games, etc. What was their motivation for giving up? How did this help them to get through it?

Talk

The Big Idea: Jesus' sacrifice on the cross was the way God dealt with the problem of sin. His example of sacrifice is the model for Christian marriage.

Recap: Last time we saw how human sin wrecks relationships. Our relationship with God is ruined because we have all turned our backs on him. And this disregard for God has a huge effect on all our relationships—so it directly affects marriage.

Let me ask you a question: What happens in any relationship where there are two people who both want to call the shots, to be in charge? *[Discuss and accept answers.]*

Inevitably, there is a power struggle. In marriage, this will result in either a life-long power struggle, or in one person becoming a bully and the other being crushed. As you can imagine, neither is ideal for a happy marriage.

Now this question is a real issue because marriage joins together two people who, up until their wedding day, have always made their own decisions. But getting married means that you won't *always* be able to have your own way.

How then can two instinctively self-pleasing people live together as husband and wife, without sooner or later wanting to escape or throttle each other? Let's read what God says in the Bible… I'll warn you in advance that these are shocking words.

> **READ: Ephesians 5 v 22-25** *(p 15 of the Study Guide)*

I told you they were shocking! But they tell us the way God designed marriage to work, with neither the stress of a power struggle or the pain of being crushed.

I've said before that marriage is a picture of the relationship between Jesus (the bridegroom) and the his people, the church (his bride). However, the relationship between Jesus and a Christian is not a relationship where each has the same role. You see, Christians willingly submit to Jesus and want to be led by Him. They trust him because they know he loves them.

Verse 24 says: *'as the church submits to Christ, so also wives should submit to their husbands in everything'*. At this point, men are usually smiling from ear to ear, and women have steam coming out of their ears! But before we go any further, we need to read v 25 as well: *'Husbands, love your wives, just as Christ loved the church and gave himself up for her'*.

We see here God's design for marriage. He wants neither a power struggle nor anyone to become a doormat. God wants men to truly love their wives. This means that the man must put his own needs and desires in second place, and seek to do what is best for his wife. A loving husband will therefore listen to his wife, and take a lead in doing what is best for her and for the marriage. And wives, knowing that their husband is seeking to love them, are to willingly submit to him in everything—even when they might have chosen to do things differently.

So the sacrifice of marriage is that wives must be willing to submit to their husbands, and husbands are to sacrifice themselves for their wives. This is the way the One who made marriage designed it to be. So [men/name], you should ask yourself: 'Is the woman I am planning to marry someone who I am prepared to sacrificially give myself up for?' And [women/name], you should ask: 'Is the man I am going to marry someone whom I am willing to entrust myself and submit to?' If, in either case, the answer is 'No' then, I would suggest, that you are either not marrying the right person, or you are not ready for marriage.

You may find this a difficult idea to accept. But in different ways, we all have to exercise authority and submit to authority—this is the way that life works. We submit to traffic rules, because we don't want to be run over on a zebra crossing. Parents lay down rules about playing with matches for children, because they love them, and don't want them to be harmed. It is no different in marriage. But the wonderful thing in marriage is that wives are to *freely* submit to someone who is seeking to love them in a self-sacrificial way—in the way that Christ loved the church—which is what we are now going to briefly turn our focus to.

> **READ: Mark 15 v 22-24, 33-34** *(p 15 of the Study Guide)*

When thinking about marriage, most people try to weigh up what sort of husband/wife they might marry, but neglect to consider what sort of husband/wife *they themselves will be*. The Bible teaches that true love is other-person centred, not self-centred; and sacrificial, not self-indulgent. It is supremely seen (as Ephesians 5 tells us) in Jesus, who selflessly gave himself up and even went to his death for his 'bride' (the church). This ultimate expression of love is the model for marriage, but it is more than that. It is actually the best news in the world for everyone (regardless of whether they are married or not), for it is the way our broken relationship with God can be restored.

Mark tells us that Jesus was crucified—that is, nailed to a cross to die. But what does this have to do with our relationship with God? One of Jesus' friends, Peter, explains...

> **READ: 1 Peter 3 v 18** *(p 15 of the Study Guide)*

Peter informs us here that Jesus' death is crucial to make us right with God. He says: 'Christ died for sins once for all, the righteous for the unrighteous, to bring you to God'.

You may remember from last time that we are 'unrighteous' because 'there is *no one* righteous, not even one ... there is *no one* who seeks God ... all have turned away.' We also heard how we will face God as our judge—and the punishment we deserve is hell—being cut off from God forever.

Peter is telling us that as Jesus died, a wonderful swap was taking place— 'the *righteous* for the *unrighteous*.' More than that, this swap was not just for a few but, 'once *for all*.' As Jesus died, he was cut off from God so that we don't have to be—which is why he cried out: 'My God, My God, why have you forsaken me?'

For the first time ever, Jesus experienced complete and utter separation from God. This was an innocent person, willingly and lovingly taking the punishment that guilty people deserve, so that they can go free.

Imagine [ladies/name] that you go off to Thailand for an exotic final holiday with 'the girls' before getting married and settling down. You have a great time, until one morning the police come to your apartment and you're arrested and charged with smuggling and supplying drugs. The evidence is all over your room. In Thailand, the penalty for dealing drugs is death. You are duly convicted, and find yourself cut off from your friends and family as you wait, helpless and hopeless, on death row.

To your astonishment, one day a guard opens the door and tells you that you are free to leave. Later, you discover the reason—your fiancé loves you so much that he has flown out to Thailand and arranged to take your place on death row. Though he is innocent of dealing drugs, he is treated as if he were guilty—and he dies in your place because he loves you. And you are treated as if you are innocent, and set free to come home to your family, where you belong.

Each one of us is guilty of turning our backs on God and living as if he isn't there. This 'sin' separates us from God, and the penalty is death—cut off forever from the One who is the source of life. However, because of his love for us, Jesus came into the world to rescue us and to set us free from that terrible penalty.

Peter finishes off his explanation by saying 'Christ died for sins ... the righteous for the unrighteous, to bring you to God.' That's why he died— he wanted to open up the way for people like us to become friends with

God, and not be his enemies any longer.

So in summary, when Jesus died on a cross, the punishment I deserve was taken by him in my place. He was cut off from God so I need never be. On the cross, Jesus was treated as if he were me, so that I can be treated as if I were him—innocent, and set free to come home to God.

Wonderfully, Jesus didn't remain dead. The Bible details very clearly that Jesus was raised to life, as promised hundreds of years before, and predicted by Jesus himself, and witnessed by over 500 people.

And this is why Christianity is doubly good news: it means that forgiveness for sin and eternal life are available from someone who has both paid the penalty of sin and defeated our great enemy, death. That's why it's the best news in the world—both our guilt before God and our mortality are dealt with.

So that's the sacrificial love of the cross. It is the supreme act of love and self-sacrifice, and that's why Christians gladly submit to Jesus as their Lord (boss) and Saviour.

It is this relationship that God holds up as the model for the way you are to relate to each other as husband and wife.

I wonder how willing you are to give yourself up or to submit to the other—when one of you wants a beach holiday and the other wants the mountains? When one wants curry and the other wants a kebab? When one wants to watch *Coronation Street* and the other wants *The Bill*? When one wants sex, and the other wants to sleep?

Most importantly, I wonder how you will respond to Jesus' love and sacrifice for you. I have to say that Christianity is great for us as individuals, but it is also a great thing for a marriage. Because Jesus shows us the essential ingredients for marriage: real love, genuine commitment, forgiveness, and self sacrifice—and he did it to bring you back to God.

Questions for discussion

★ *Did you realise how much God loves you? What is remarkable about the love he shows us at the cross?*

★ *Why do you think Peter emphasises that Jesus was 'righteous' ie: he had never done anything wrong himself?*

Discuss their responses to these questions.

Homework

• Encourage the couples to meet again during the week to talk through the question and tips on page 16.

• Tell them to also write down separately their answers to the questions on page 17.

• Provide for them a copy of the wedding service you will use. Ask them to read through it and talk about what they think the vows mean.

Your notes

Your notes

the promises

Write down what you think about the Marriage 'deal':

- Your 'vows' are of the utmost seriousness (as the wedding service puts it, they are 'solemn'). You will make them to each other before God.

- You will publicly declare your willingness to enter into marriage with each other, before your families and friends.

- Your commitment is unconditional: *'For better, for worse; for richer, for poorer; in sickness and in health ...'.*

- You will say *'I will'*, not *'I do'!* Your commitment is for life: *'to love and to cherish, until death us do part'.*

If this isn't for you, don't be afraid to pull out of this deal BEFORE you make the commitment.

the promise of God

John 3 v 36
Whoever believes in the Son has eternal life,
but whoever rejects the Son will not see life,
for God's wrath remains on him.

OPTION 1: REJECT JESUS

- Continue to live life my own way (with me in charge).

- Continue to ignore God and what he has done for us in the person of Jesus.

- Continue to think that I know better than God.

- Remain unforgiven and facing God's right anger at my sin.

- Cut off from God... forever

OPTION 2: BELIEVE IN JESUS

- Trust Jesus as your Saviour, knowing that He has paid the penalty for your sin.

- Receive eternal life and forgiveness as a free gift—and so be in a right relationship with God.

- Live with Jesus as the boss of your life ('Lord').

THE FORK IN THE ROAD

- Which way are you going?

Questions for discussion:

★ *What's your reaction to what you are required to promise to each other?*

_____

_____

★ *Is there anything that you're not sure about?*

_____

★ *What's your reaction to the promise of God?*

_____

★ *Is there anything stopping you from believing in Jesus?*

_____

A prayer for when you are ready:

Dear God,

I know I don't deserve to be accepted by you.

I am guilty of ignoring you and I need forgiveness.

Thank you that Jesus died for me so that I can be forgiven.

Thank you that he rose from the dead to give me new life.

Please come into my life—forgive me and change me.

And help me to live with Jesus as my Lord and Saviour.

Amen.

to think about together...

The promises you will make on your wedding day are life-long: *'...for better for worse, for richer for poorer, in sickness and in health, till death us do part...'*

1. *How will you deal with the situation when you find yourself attracted to someone else?*

2. *There may be times, sometimes prolonged, when sickness, or simply the tiredness that comes with work or young children, will mean that sex is off the agenda. How will you cope with that in a way that draws you together, rather than pushes you apart?*

TOP TIPS

★ **Outside attractions**
Be honest! Share inappropriate feelings of attraction with someone else (preferably your spouse, but if not, then a trusted friend of the same sex). This will often help the feelings to die down.

★ **Money**
Joint accounts or separate? There is no right or wrong way to organise your finances: do a mini-survey of some married friends (or your parents) to find out how they organise things—and the advantages and disadvantages of their approach. Decide what will work for you.

★ **Debt**
Money is often a major source of problems in marriage. If you are in debt, do talk together and get good advice about how you can get out of it. Problems only get worse if you remain silent.

the promises

Welcome

121

- Check that the couple have discussed the material on pages 16 and 17 of the Study Guide. Again, it may have raised important issues about the nature of the marriage commitment, that will need discussing openly and honestly.

group

- As a start-up exercise, ask couples to talk about promises they have made to themselves, or to other people that they have both kept and broken. Why did they break them? What were the consequences?

Talk

The Big Idea: God promises eternal life and a new start to anyone who believes in his Son. It's a rock-solid promise that will not be broken. This is the type of promise made in marriage.

Whenever you enter into a contract with someone, it's important to read the small print so that you know what the whole deal is—and what you can expect if something goes wrong. In a few weeks time, you will be entering into a special kind of contract with each other. You are going to make some very serious promises—they are called 'vows' because they are of the utmost seriousness ('solemn'), and you will say them to each other before God.

Well, it's very important before you do that, to fully understand what the deal is with marriage—what are you committing yourself to—and what the score is when things go wrong—as they do in all marriages.

On the 'big day', having declared individually your willingness to marry each other, you will then publicly state how things will be from that day on. You will vow to stick together, 'for better, for worse; for richer, for poorer; in sickness, and in health'.

Those short simple phrases are huge and far-reaching in a way that you may not be able to imagine today. You will only realise their extent when you're up against it, when you hit a rough patch, when you're not sure you want to be married (at least, not to each other), when one of you is ill for a long time and the other has to care and cook and clean; when one of you does something that is harmful to your relationship.

You see, the promises that you will make are long term. That vow you will make continues with the words 'to love and to cherish, *till death us do part'*. You are in effect saying to each other: 'Whatever life throws at us, whatever happens (better or worse), I'm going to be committed to you and love you—*for life.'*

So when I ask you on your wedding day if you are willing to take the other as your husband/wife, I'm really asking you if you are willing to make that level of commitment. And if you are, you will reply: *'I will'*.

You won't say *'I do'* which Hollywood seems to insert into weddings at this point. Anyone can say 'I do' on one single day when their partner is looking like a million dollars. But you are required to say: *'I will'*. It's an answer which points to the future—to a time when you like the look of someone else, or perhaps when your spouse won't look great, when they've put on 20lbs, or when, for whatever reason, they are not able to be what you would like them to be, or provide what you would like them to provide. But you will still love them and remain committed to them.

That is what marriage is—unconditional, total commitment—for life. And that is what you will promise to each other when you make those vows.

If you're not sure that this is for you, it is best to pull out of this contract before you say those words, and I will support you and help you if you decide to do that.

One of the reasons that marriage is for life is because marriage reflects God's relationship with his people. God is utterly faithful to his people. He hates adultery, not least because he is a faithful God. And so when God makes a promise, he always keeps it. And we're going to spend a few minutes now considering one of the promises that God makes:

Recap: So far, we have seen that God made everything (including marriage) and that he is therefore in charge. We also saw that he actually came into the world in the person of Jesus.

However, we saw in Session 2 that we have all ignored God and his right to be in charge of us—we think we know best—and that is why the world and our lives are in such a mess, and why our relationships with God and each other are broken. One day, God will judge us and punish those who insist on ignoring him.

Thankfully, that's not all. Last time we heard how Jesus came into the world to rescue us. Dying on a cross, he was cut off from God in our place. But more than that, Jesus rose from the dead, which means that he not only offers us forgiveness and a relationship with God through his death, but also eternal life through his resurrection.

It leaves us with a choice. The Bible says we have two options…

❯ READ: John 3 v 36 *(p 18 of the Study Guide)*

1. Reject Jesus. This means to continue living our own way—thinking we know better than God and so living our lives without him. Sadly, this is what so many people choose to do—but it's a huge mistake…

Jesus tells us why in that verse: it's a mistake because 'God's wrath remains' on us. 'Wrath' is God's right, fair, and controlled anger at our rebellion against him. Jesus is saying that if we choose to ignore his rescue, then God will rightly remain angry with us, and we will not have the life or forgiveness that he offers to those who believe and trust in him.

It makes sense, doesn't it? If we are unwilling to accept that Jesus has taken the rap for us, then we'll have to take it ourselves. And those who ignore Jesus will be condemned for rejecting his right as God to rule over our lives. They will get what they deserve and what they have chosen— eternity cut off from God—what the Bible calls hell.

What I have just described is terrible and terrifying, but it would be wrong to hide it. There is another option...

2. Believe in Jesus. For those who realise that they are living in God's world but ignoring him, God holds out this life-line and promise. He says: 'If you believe in my Son, you will have eternal life'. Why? Well, because he accepts his Son's death as payment for our sin. He is therefore able to forgive us, and no longer regard us as rebels, but as his children.

Believing in Jesus means two things...

First, it means trusting in what Jesus did on the cross—trusting that by his death my sin is dealt with and I can be forgiven and put right with God.

Secondly, it means trusting Jesus as Lord (or 'Boss')—recognising that as Lord and God, Jesus is in charge of everything. Therefore, rather than living for myself, I will want Jesus to be in charge of every part of my life—how I spend my time, how I conduct my marriage and all other relationships, how I behave, my attitude to money, sex, booze, children—everything.

Those two options could not be more different: rejecting Jesus and living for myself, or believing in Jesus and living for him. This brings us to a sort of fork in the road, because everyone at some point has to decide which way they are going to live. By doing nothing, you are still rejecting Jesus.

Obviously, we live in a world where rejecting God is the norm. So believing in Jesus is not easy. But that does not mean it's wrong. On the contrary, one day Jesus will be our judge, and John 3 v 36 tells us that our response to Jesus *now* makes the difference between eternal life *then* or God remaining angry with us *for ever*.

In summary, believing in Jesus brings the promise of forgiveness and eternal life (which is what we all crave in our hearts), and a right relationship with the God who made us.

And it is that relationship with God through Jesus that is actually the key to a great marriage. It is Jesus who shows a husband and wife how to relate to each other—in a truly loving, sacrificial, and committed way.

More than that, if you cast your mind back to our first two sessions, you may remember that the first 'domestic' between husband and wife came about when the man and woman ignored God and broke their relation-ship with him. Their relationship with each other was much better before they did that. Well, Jesus offers us the chance to get right with God. And I would suggest that there is no better preparation for married life than getting put right with the God who made you and who is the author of marriage.

'Whoever believes in the Son has eternal life, but whoever rejects the Son will not see life, for God's wrath remains on him'.

That's the promise of God. That is the commitment God makes to us. I wonder if, as you embark on a new life together, you want the new life, the eternal life that Jesus holds out to those who believe in Him. It's basi-cally an offer to be a guest at the best wedding reception ever—the wed-ding of the model bridegroom (Jesus Christ) to his bride (the church) in Heaven. It's going to be a great party—I do hope you'll be there!

Questions for discussion

★ What is your reaction to what you are required to promise to each other?
★ Is there anything that you are unsure about?
★ What's your reaction to the promise of God?
★ Is there anything stopping you from believing in Jesus?

Discuss their responses to these questions, and any other issues that they have about the wedding.

• Emphasise the importance of the statement at the foot of page 17 in their Study Guide. It is no shame to pull out, or to delay the wedding, if there are serious issues to deal with. It is the loving thing to do if you are unsure, or if you know that you will not be able to keep the promises in the wedding vows.

Homework

• Ask the couple to *each* fill in the feedback form, and send it to you.

• Finalise plans and check dates for the rehearsal/wedding.

• Encourage them to contact you if there is anything else that they need to discuss before or after the wedding.

• Draw their attention to the book list, and perhaps offer to source a book for them if they are interested.

Your notes

Your notes

evaluation form

Please tick the appropriate answers. Please feel free not to answer all or even any of the questions. Do be honest and frank.

Name _____

1. *How would you say this course has made you think differently as you have prepared for your marriage?*

_____

_____

2. *Which aspect have you most enjoyed?*

_____

3. *Which part have you least enjoyed?*

_____

_____

4. *Are there any areas that were not touched upon that you would have found helpful?*

_____

_____

5. *Before you began this course, how would you have described yourself?*
   - ☐ I didn't believe in God
   - ☐ I wasn't sure if God existed or not
   - ☐ I believed in God but not in Jesus
   - ☐ A Christian (personally committed to Jesus)
   - ☐ Something else _____

6. *Where would you say you stand now in relation to Jesus?*

☐ I have genuinely repented and come to believe in Jesus as my Lord and Saviour

☐ I am interested in learning more but, as yet, not ready to believe in Jesus as Lord and Saviour.

☐ Other _____

7. *If you have not believed in Jesus as your personal Saviour, what do you think is stopping you?*

_____

_____

8. *Are there any questions for which you would still like an answer?*

_____

_____

_____

_____

_____

_____

10. *Would you like to join a course that explores the meaning of the Christian faith in greater depth?*

☐ Yes

☐ No

Please return this form to the person who did the course with you.

after the course

The wedding day

Following **Preparing for Marriage**, there will (probably) be a wedding day for the couples you have been preparing. This is another opportunity to say something useful about the Lord Jesus.

Couples who are not Christians will probably require some help in choosing a Bible reading (if they haven't already decided that it will be 1Corinthians 13!) You might suggest Ephesians 5 v 21-33—the beginning of which they will remember from Session 3. Other passages to consider would be Philippians 2 v 1-11, 1 John 4 v 7-17, or Revelation 21 v 1-7, There are others too, but make sure that you are going to be able to say something worthwhile about Jesus—and get to it reasonably quickly because time is short at a non-Christian wedding, in terms of concentration and expectation of those present.

After the wedding

Beyond the wedding day it would be very easy to lose contact with each couple—I know because I've done it—and you probably have too. It occurred to me recently that I only have to order a book from a catalogue or online, and I will be sent future catalogues at least four times a year (more online), or information about other books or services which may interest me… and sometimes, I take the bait! By the end of a four-session preparation course, we will (hopefully!) have a far better relationship with those who have done the course than a mail-order company has with its customers. Why then do we forget people, and not let them know of other things at church which may interest them?

Here are a couple of suggestions. Although it's easy to lose contact, it is also easy to keep a wedding diary of the couples we have married and when. With that information readily at hand, we can post or personally deliver invitations to couples, inviting them to join us at guest services— Easter, Remembrance day, Christmas, Mother's/Father's Day—anytime when you are particularly doing something for those who are not

Christians. Make sure they are sent information about *Christianity Explored*, or whatever evangelistic course that you run. And if your church runs a marriage course, those who have been married in your church should be top of the list for information and invitations. In addition, why not invite each couple to church on the Sunday nearest to their anniversary?—Their first anniversary will probably be on a Sunday, and it would be so easy to have a simple letter that wishes them a happy anniversary and invites them to your Sunday meeting on that day.

These are just simple and easy ways to make the most of the opportunity which conducting weddings provides. And given that there is a lot going on in a person's life when they are preparing for marriage, it may be that the chance to hear about Jesus at a more relaxed time will bear more fruit. Let's grasp the opportunity—it's there for the taking!

SEX
One Flesh
Amelia & Greg Clarke (Matthias Media)

This friendly, enjoyable and highly informative introduction to sex in marriage explains the Bible's teaching on sex, the practicalities of beginning a sexual relationship, and the kinds of problems which commonly emerge for couples. It also considers the consequences of sexual sin for a married couple.

MARRIAGE
God, Sex and Marriage
John Richardson (The Good Book Company)

A short introduction to the big issues from the pages of the New Testament.

The Diamond Marriage
Simon Vibert (Christian Focus Publications)

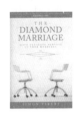

How can joy in marriage be revived? This biblical perspective on marriage is packed with insight, wisdom and wit.

Don't they make a lovely couple?
John & Anne Benton (CFP)

Six important questions for couples to work through. Short and highly readable.

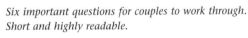

These titles are available from your local Christian bookshop, or by visiting www.thegoodbook.co.uk

UNDERSTANDING THE CHRISTIAN FAITH

The Bible!

No better place to start than by reading one of the gospels—we recommend Luke—and to start thinking about who Jesus is, and what he has done. Find a modern translation like the NIV, and read it in small sections, writing down your questions and observations to discuss with your partner, or with an established Christian.

A Fresh Start
John Chapman (The Good Book Company)

An honest and down-to-earth read about: just what God has done for us through his son, Jesus; how we can know it is true; what the alternatives are; and what we should do about it.

Christianity Explored
Rico Tice (The Good Book Company)

Drawing from the Gospel of Mark, this book explores who Jesus was, what his aims were, and what it means to follow him. Concise, entertaining and honest, it's an ideal book for anyone with little or no experience of Christianity.

These titles are available from your local Christian bookshop, or by visiting www.thegoodbook.co.uk